# You Always Matter

# Also by Lisa Aré Wulf

**Hidden in God's Heart**
**40 Reflections to Draw You Close to Christ**


**Reaching for God's Hand**
**40 Reflections to Deepen Your Faith Journey**


**Enfolded in God's Arms**
**40 Reflections to Embrace Your Inner Healing**


**On a Quest for Christ**
**Tracing the Footsteps of Your Spiritual Journey**



For more information on these titles
or to sign up for Lisa's e-newsletter,
please go to LisaAreWulf.com

# You Always Matter

# Resting in God's Tender Embrace

## by Lisa Aré Wulf

**"You're Worth It"
Devotional Series**

**Spiritual Formation House
Colorado Springs, Colorado**

# Large Print Edition

Cover Design by Fresh Vision Design
Interior Design by Wood Nymph Creations
Cover Graphic by EnginKorkmaz (Depositphotos.com)
Interior Graphic by Kareemovic_Kareemov1000 (Depositphotos.com)
Author Photograph by Katie Corinne Photography
Two stories used by permission from Rev. Dr. Daniel Holt

Library of Congress Control Number 2024913036

Large Print: 978-1-938042-29-4

Published by Spiritual Formation House
3154 Vickers Drive
Colorado Springs, CO 80918
SpiritualFormationHouse.com

Printed in the United States of America

# Contents

# Our Journey Begins

## Opening Words

*The Lord will rejoice over you with gladness; he will quiet you by his love; he will exult over you with loud singing.  Zephaniah 3:17b*

Our mission—should we choose to accept it—is to live out the truth of who we are.

This is a bold statement, especially for those of us who feel unsure. Unsure of our worth. Unsure of our value. Unsure of life itself.

But God never intended to paint our world in such dreary colors. No, he created us in his image. We are good—just slightly smudged around the edges.

Why not rub out those spots and shine up your spirit? As you ponder these 30 reflections, you will:

- Receive new inspiration to see yourself differently.

- Embrace the ability to recognize your worth.

- Envelop your soul in scripture and prayer.

On our trek, we'll discover what Jesus already knows. We matter. Who we are makes a difference. After all, God rejoices over us with singing. We must be special.

It's time to begin our adventure. Along the way, we may identify obstacles that hinder our growth. We might explore fresh ways to affirm our value. Best of all, Jesus promises a lovely serenade as we walk the path of life together. Take my hand. Let's get moving.

# A Snippet of Ribbon

## Reflection 1

*For the Lord sees not as man sees: man looks on the outward appearance, but the Lord looks on the heart. 1 Samuel 16:7b*

Once upon a time, an unknown candidate burst onto the political scene to win a local election. That was me. My years on city council were memorable, filled with meaningful work and tender moments.

Each meeting began with a special time of listening. We encouraged citizens to speak to the council on any subject for five minutes. One encounter remains etched in my mind.

A gentleman approached the podium with nine small blue ribbons. After a few short remarks, he handed one to each council member. The embossed gold lettering read, "Who I Am Makes a Difference." Deeply touched, I took the ribbon home and taped it to my bedroom mirror. That little blue bit of inspiration greeted me each morning. I still have it.

Whenever I doubted myself, this ribbon boosted my confidence and reminded me I was a person of value. It helped me break free from hurtful assumptions about myself. It revealed my worth.

This may be a common feeling. We wonder if our lives matter at all. We're afraid we don't have what it takes to succeed or that we're not special enough to be loved.

Nothing could be further from the truth. Whatever our challenges, we matter. Just ask Jesus. He doesn't judge by the world's standards. With a loving gaze and a tender smile, he inspires every soul to shine.

*It is he who made us, and we are his; we are his people, and the sheep of his pasture.*
*Psalm 100:3b*

## You Always Matter

Why was this ribbon so significant? Why did I keep it for decades? Perhaps this tiny blue banner showed me I had value, regardless of my circumstances. And what does a person of value do? Make a difference, of course. Each day, I build a legacy that celebrates the core of who I am.

This lesson is also for you. Never forget that the ribbon confirms your value, too. How about making one for yourself and taping it to your mirror? I'll bet Jesus would be delighted.

## Ponder and Pray

When have you doubted your worth, but later recognized your true value?

Were you able to hold on to your new belief? Why or why not?

How can you and God create a more uplifting mindset?

*Lord, some days I struggle and desperately want to believe I'm okay. Then, right on cue, you send me the love and encouragement I need. Help me know that who I am matters. Amen.*

# Rocky Road

## Reflection 2

*Behold, God is my helper; the Lord is the upholder of my life. Psalm 54:4*

New school. New semester. New possibilities.

Eager students swarmed the college, settling in for another term. But this freshman faced a new challenge—his first online course. Mastering the world of computer learning is daunting at best. No wonder he was a little queasy.

His initial task was to introduce himself to his virtual classmates on a discussion board. Wanting to liven things up a bit, the professor asked each student to name a favorite ice cream. The young man pondered his answer.

How could he tie his construction management studies to an ice cream choice? At last, he hit on a unique way to declare his love of Rocky Road, a sweet treat indeed.

"Life is a rocky road, but if you have a good suspension system, you'll never notice how rough the road really is."

How true. But what is a good suspension system? Is it money, possessions, family, or friends? These are all important and often serve this purpose. But what if they fail, especially when we need them most? Then we're left to face the rough road alone. Or are we?

There's one suspension system that is always there and never lets us down. Jesus. The road ahead may be choppy, but riding beside him softens the bumps. And who knows—maybe he'll treat us to a yummy ice cream cone along the way. Rocky Road anyone?

*I sought the Lord, and he answered me and delivered me from all my fears.  Psalm 34:4*

## You Always Matter

A reliable suspension system is essential for both cars and people. But sometimes we hit potholes. Or crucial parts fall off. Or entire systems break down. My shock absorbers have been rather unreliable from time to time. But I am grateful to my mechanic, Jesus. Thanks to his excellent alignment services, enjoyable road trips are back in my future.

And here's the exciting part for you. It's never too late to create a solid foundation. No matter how alone or splintered you feel, Jesus offers a steady hand to help build a strong new life.

## Ponder and Pray

Does your suspension system need a bit of "shoring up?" In what ways?

How might you do that?

What guidance would Jesus give you?


*Lord, when I compare myself to others, I feel so discouraged. They seem to have it all together and I don't. But I'm forgetting a crucial fact. You love me just as I am, and our team is building a super strong suspension system. So, let's get moving. Amen.*

# The Buzz About Bees

## Reflection 3

*Our help is in the name of the Lord, who made heaven and earth. Psalm 124:8*

Bees are buzzing around social media. Let this adaptation of an anonymous tale stir your heart.

Beekeeping was his passion. One day, while on the verge of pouring fresh honey into a bucket, his son grabbed his sleeve. "Look," the boy said. "Three little bees are trapped on top. They're drowning! Can't we save them?"

Sure enough. In a desperate fight for survival, the tiny bees were sinking fast. His father scooped them into a small bowl, doubting the insects would survive.

But a surprise awaited. In a stealth move, sister bees swarmed in to clean off the frantic trio. Two had already recovered and flown away. The last baby bee finally broke free and escaped.

A lovely story, and so helpful during tough times. When we're struggling, who wouldn't want phone calls brimming with encouragement, food brought by a friend, or the loving prayers of our community?

But what if our aid is a bit tardy? We're left to tackle trouble all alone—a terrifying thought. Don't worry. Help is on the way. We just don't see it yet.

Looking back, we remember people who lent a hand when we least expected it. Maybe they emerged out of nowhere. Or perhaps they were there all along, silently waiting to be asked. Either way, they were by our side.

This saga is about helpers. They are everywhere. So be on the lookout. And who is the ultimate helper? Jesus, of course.

*For you have been my help, and in the shadow of your wings I will sing for joy.  Psalm 63:7*

## You Always Matter

How delightful to be part of a "hive" eagerly offering assistance in a crisis. But why would anyone do that for me? Okay, I'm too negative. Let's try again. Why wouldn't they? Jesus provides an answer to every difficulty. I just need to hang on until it arrives.

You might believe you're not important enough for someone to lend a hand. But you are mistaken. You deserve the same care and attention as the little bees. So, watch for the helpers. They are all around you.

## Ponder and Pray

When have you faced a challenging situation by yourself?

Did you receive support from an unexpected source? Who was it?

How could you strengthen your faith that God is there for you?

*Lord, sometimes I feel so isolated, with no hand to grasp in distress. It's hard to find solutions. But you always provide them, right before my eyes. Let's discover my helpers together. Amen.*

# Brave Little Leaf

## Reflection 4

*Be strong, and let your heart take courage, all you who wait for the Lord!  Psalm 31:24*

As the sun set over the mountains, my hot tub beckoned. Fed up with unsolvable problems, I was overwhelmed, exhausted, and ready to quit. Yet when the warm water caressed my tired limbs, chaos faded as peace settled in.

Tucked away in the side yard, my hot tub refuge was exposed to wind, rain, and snow. An old tree overlooked the patio. As I indulged in my nightly soak, the seasons slowly passed. In summer, its foliage was lush and green. One by one, the leaves began to drop as fall inched closer. When winter arrived, the tree stood bare.

Bare, except for one small leaf that wouldn't give up. Wilted and limp, it clung to the tree, refusing to let go. I studied that leaf through months of frost and chill. What kept it attached to the branch? Was it brave? Was it determined? Whatever the reason, I admired the tiny leaf.

Spring finally rolled around. Fresh growth appeared and the little leaf fell at last. I never saw it again, yet its memory lingered.

Will we hang on like that leaf despite difficulty and struggle? Will we persevere no matter what? The courageous little leaf encourages us to be brave. After all, if a leaf can persist, so can we.

Let's strive each day to fulfill our destiny, like the tiny leaf. And as our last moment approaches, we'll fall ever so gently into God's embrace. What a lovely place to rest.

*Fear not, for I am with you; be not dismayed, for I am your God.  Isaiah 41:10a*

## You Always Matter

As I stepped into the swirling water each evening, I hoped I would find my mini friend still hanging on. That plucky leaf captivated my soul. Despite the bleak winter chill, it never quit. The brave little leaf lifted my spirit as it nurtured my heart. I moved forward again with renewed confidence and strength.

When you think your life doesn't matter, remember that leaf. It didn't give up, even as it crackled and curled. The leaf recognized its worth. And so should you.

## Ponder and Pray

Do you ever feel like giving up?

How might you follow the example of the tiny leaf?

Where do you see God's helping hand?


*Lord, there are days when it's tough to keep going. Life seems overwhelming and I need a fresh start. Teach me to appreciate my value, like that small leaf. Show me that the world needs me. Be with me today and always. Amen.*

# Divine Decor
## Reflection 5

*And my God will supply every need of yours according to his riches in glory in Christ Jesus. Philippians 4:19*

Dreary gloom lingers over her bed. In her dream, she huddles in a bare one-room shack. A single lightbulb dangles from a wire in the rafters. The space is dark and filled with despair. Streaks of grime stain the faded walls and shattered glass mars the only window.

Suddenly Jesus arrives, driving a pickup. He hops out and strides briskly into her house. After a quick glance, he announces, "You need an interior decorator!"

Climbing aboard his truck, he sorts through his inventory, choosing the perfect decor. Carrying in load after load, he transforms her home. Comfy couches rest on a thick rug while cheery curtains blow in the breeze. An elegant chandelier hangs above, reflecting stylish artwork on the bright accent walls. He even fixes the windowpane.

His job complete, Jesus jumps back into his pickup. With a friendly wave goodbye, he drives on to his next stop.

Is this a dream? Or reality? Many of us live in bleak circumstances in our own minds. Perhaps this is all we believe we are worth. Life could be better. But we're clueless about how to fix it.

We deserve much more than a rundown shack. It's time to invite Jesus, the master decorator, into our hearts. Watch as he sweeps away the cobwebs and creates a cozy little abode. Call him today. He'll be right over.

*For nothing will be impossible with God.*
*Luke 1:37*

## You Always Matter

I lived in that house for years—at least in my mind. Nobody ever suspected my secret. Hey, I looked like I had it all together. But I didn't. Then Jesus, the divine decorator, visited me one day in my prayers. Beauty and abundance came within reach. After a while, I moved out of that dismal dwelling forever.

What about you? Does a lovely and fulfilling life seem out of reach? Guess what—it's not. Why not release those limiting thoughts and embrace peace, tranquility, and grace?

## Ponder and Pray

Have you been stuck in a mindset of scarcity, believing you're not worth it? Describe.

Now picture a delightful and joyful reality. What do you see?

How could you and Jesus create this together?


*Lord, my world feels small and a rich, satisfying life seems beyond my grasp. All my options appear constricted and narrow. But I know you have exciting plans for me, so please help me recognize my true value. Side by side, we'll build a fantastic future. Amen.*

# Let's Cross Over
## Reflection 6

*The Lord will keep your going out and your coming in from this time forth and forevermore.*
*Psalm 121:8*

You speak Italian, right? What! You don't? Well, that's okay. I'll give you a hint. As our story's tourist learned, "Attraversiamo" is a handy phrase for maneuvering through crowded streets.

Traffic in Rome is crazy. Because the boulevards are wide, pedestrians must cross multiple lanes packed with oncoming cars. Foot travelers have the right-of-way. Yet many drivers either forget or ignore that fact. It's no wonder our tourist was flustered.

She stood on the street corner, searching for the safest route across the intersection. A friendly Roman resident offered this advice. "Just start walking, keep up a steady pace, and you'll get to the other side." Fearful but determined, she began to walk. One by one, the vehicles dodged around her. Soon she arrived at the opposite corner, safe and sound.

Traffic and life have much in common. Perhaps we sense God's calling in a certain direction. What should we do? Will we succeed? These concerns are valid. But sometimes we just need to trust, step off the curb, and walk.

And here's a special bonus. As we navigate our path, close friends and family may find insight and inspiration. Our courage could bring a new direction and purpose to their lives, too.

But no matter what, we can't forget Jesus. He's right beside us, directing traffic as we venture out in faith.

*For I, the Lord your God, hold your right hand; it is I who say to you, "Fear not, I am the one who helps you." Isaiah 41:13*

## You Always Matter

As I take on new challenges, I'm often unsure. Are the tasks too hard? Will everything work out? These tough questions could stop anyone. Crossing over requires faith, determination, and self-compassion. And it's not always successful. Yet even if I fall a bit short, exciting opportunities for growth are sure to appear.

Knowing your worth is vital. And yes, stepping into unfamiliar territory can be frightening. But remember, you have what it takes regardless of what lies ahead. Hey world, get ready for an epic crossover.

## Ponder and Pray

Are you facing a crossing over situation?

How can you keep moving forward?

God is with you. Do you sense his presence?


*Lord, walking through oncoming traffic is scary. So many cars, so much confusion. That's how I feel about predicaments in my life. But I can't stay in one place forever. It's time to cross over. Please walk with me. With you as my navigator, we'll do wonderful things. Amen.*

# Going Home
## Reflection 7

*For every house is built by someone, but the builder of all things is God.  Hebrews 3:4*

Bargains. I love them. And nothing beats a Christmas discount! Last year's holiday hunt yielded a cute little vacuum robot, vastly marked down. I plopped him into the virtual shopping cart and clicked the "buy" button. Soon, he was speeding to his new home.

A few days later, the package arrived. Free from his wrappings, my new vacuum was ready for action. I named him Jeeves, a common name for a butler—or in this case, a robot.

Jeeves is a delightful addition to my family. He works hard, has a knack for finding dirt, is quite pleasant, and says hi as he chugs past. But one feature especially intrigues me. He always knows where his home is.

After Jeeves finishes his work, I press a button on his remote control, and he heads for his base. Wherever he may be, the radar leads him home. He may search for a bit, but he always finds his way back.

It's the same with God. He's our home base. We may have a busy schedule. We may be exhausted and worn out. We may face countless challenges and difficulties. Yet Jesus, our central hub, is always there. His love provides a safe haven that never changes.

Our home base is eager to welcome us anytime, no matter what. So, let's head to the docking station for a recharge. I'll meet you there.

*My people will abide in a peaceful habitation,
in secure dwellings, and in quiet resting places.
Isaiah 32:18*

## You Always Matter

Sometimes I'm not sure where my home is. Yes, I know my address. But where is my spiritual home? Where do I belong? Where am I safe? Definitely tough questions for those who struggle. The answer could be family. Or friends. Or none of the above. But who always values us? You guessed it—God.

What about you? Care to join Jesus for a few moments? Allow his gentle presence to help you find rest and tranquility. With him, you are always at home.

## Ponder and Pray

When have you felt lost, either physically or emotionally?

How did you find your way back home?

Was Jesus with you? How could you tell?

*Lord, many times I feel stuck and stranded on a road going nowhere. I'm certain there's a path toward peace, safety, and understanding. But where is it? I can't find it alone. Hold my hand and help me accept the love you offer every moment. Guide me home once again. Amen.*

# Garage Sailing
## Reflection 8

*He heals the brokenhearted and binds up their wounds.  Psalm 147:3*

What do garage sale junkies live for? Nabbing hidden treasure, of course. One true "garage sailor" packed in tons of sales every weekend. These adventures were usually disappointing. Yet, at times, he encountered something truly astonishing.

One such discovery awaited him at a Saturday event—a bona fide ball and chain. You know, the kind prisoners wore back in the old days. The heavy black metal piece was a super spooky find.

He bought the set right away and drove home, wondering how it would feel to wear such a contraption. The weight of the shackle would surely cause sore and bleeding ankles. Should the prisoner attempt to flee, the ball may swing, causing further harm. The captive was helpless, dejected, and humiliated.

Notice how similar this is to our own lives? Earlier memories and events weigh us down, inflicting lasting suffering. The past shackles our souls, preventing us from finding healing despite our best efforts. We may seem cheerful on the outside, but we are not okay.

Yet comfort and renewal are always possible. Help is on the way to guide and support our journey to wellness. As we cast aside our ball and chain, the feet of our inner world cease to bleed.

Our emotional and spiritual legs are no longer bruised. And when we look for helpers, someone stands out above the rest. It's Jesus.

*O Lord my God, I cried to you for help, and you have healed me.  Psalm 30:2*

## You Always Matter

Releasing the grip of the past is a battle. Try as I might, pesky thoughts continue to haunt me and influence my life. How tiresome. I just want to be free. I long to be light and joyful. But a black metal monstrosity holds me back. Am I strong enough to throw off that ball and chain? You bet. And today's the day.

How about you? Don't let your spirit languish, held back by heavy iron shackles. Escape those constraints. Once you do, you'll see friends waiting and eager to join your journey, especially Jesus.

## Ponder and Pray

Do painful memories ever shackle you so you can't move ahead? When?

How do these thoughts hinder your hopes of a happy life?

Where do you sense God's help?

*Lord, dragging around a ball and chain is no fun. My body aches and my heart feels stifled. This pain must stop—now! Please unlock my shackles and fling them far away. Then you and I will stroll side by side, free forever. Amen.*

# Listen

## Reflection 9

*This is my commandment, that you love one another as I have loved you.  John 15:12*

"The most basic and powerful way to connect to another person is to listen. Just listen. Perhaps the most important thing we ever give each other is our attention. ... A loving silence often has far more power to heal and to connect than the most well-intentioned words." Rachel Naomi Remen

When her husband's good friend passed away unexpectedly, she longed to comfort his widow. But she felt like just a casual acquaintance since they barely knew each other. What could she say? Would the conversation be helpful? She scoured the web for guidance and gathered her courage, determined to be a caring and supportive listener.

She scheduled a morning date at a coffee shop, hoping the get-together would go well. They talked about lots of subjects. Sometimes it was life as a widow. Sometimes it was something else. But she let her new friend take the lead.

Compassionate listening provides a healing space, a space to be heard, and a space free from judgement. The speaker feels safe, understood, and encouraged. By investing in relationships, we work through and heal emotional pain. Nothing compares to the gift of a kind and caring ear.

When we show how much we care by listening, our own thoughts and feelings may remain unspoken. Not to worry. We have plenty of time for that later. For now, let's remember Jesus spends hours listening to us. Why not pass it on?

*Therefore encourage one another and build one another up.  1 Thessalonians 5:11a*

## You Always Matter

Sometimes I doubt my ability as a listener. Do I slip up? Do I make mistakes? I try hard but worry my skills aren't quite up to par. But is that true? No. This isn't a contest to be crowned "best listener." Rather, it's an act of friendship and understanding. The goal is a deep and mutual relationship.

It's the same for you. Your heart is already brimming with compassion. Your gesture of listening to another refreshes and strengthens both souls. And don't forget, Jesus is holding hands with you both.

## Ponder and Pray

Have you ever tried to listen to a struggling friend? How did it go?

Does deep listening come easy to you, or is this a challenge? Why?

How could God help build your skills and your relationships?

*Lord, am I a good listener? Who knows? Despite my best efforts, supporting a hurting person can be difficult. Please guide me as I learn to slow down and listen—truly listen. Amen.*

# By the Pond
## Reflection 10

*My help comes from the Lord, who made heaven and earth.  Psalm 121:2*

The retreat center landscape sparkled in the morning sun. Out for an early walk, I strolled past three deer munching their breakfast grass. Soon, my destination was in sight—a small pond tucked away in the glade. In the middle, a fountain spewed water high in the air. Deep in thought, I stopped to rest on a rickety bench. Peace and serenity washed over me as the sound of the spray filled my senses.

Later, I continued my trek. Rounding the corner, I discovered a secret surprise at the rear of the pond. A hose. Turns out, this was an artificial pool. A man-made device replenished it every day with water from somewhere else.

That pond is a reflection of our lives. Some days, we're smart, successful folks with a plan. Other days, we're unsure and afraid of failure. Either way, we know it's all up to us. Or is it? What fuels our efforts? Our own power or something else?

Jesus backfills our lives, just like the hose brought water to the pond. When our throats are parched and dry, he's there offering comfort and support. As we embark on new projects or plan exciting events, there he is again, pouring energy into our souls.

Not only does this sacred hose sustain us, but it also provides water to share. Why not offer a drink to a thirsty traveler along the road? Together, we can truly make a difference.

*Trust in the Lord forever, for the Lord God is an everlasting rock.  Isaiah 26:4*

## You Always Matter

Sometimes I feel overwhelmed and swamped with burdens too heavy to carry. Today's task demands immediate attention. Tomorrow's work is crucial. It never ends and then fear sets in, sliding everything downhill. What if I'm not good enough? What if I fail? It's comforting to know I'm on God's irrigation system that never gets clogged.

This holds true for you, as well. Don't worry, Jesus is backfilling your life, too. Whatever happens, he's there to replenish your special pond. His water supply is endless.

## Ponder and Pray

Do you ever feel drained, like you just can't go on? When?

Have you stopped to consider where your strength comes from?

How can you tap into Jesus?

*Lord, when doubt takes over, it's easy to be discouraged about myself and my worth. But I'm forgetting about your special hose, pouring courage into me every day. Help me discover you in the background, supporting and encouraging me. Keep my pond full forever. Amen.*

# Clutter Buster

## Reflection 11

*Create in me a clean heart, O God, and renew a right spirit within me.  Psalm 51:10*

"Clutter is invading our church at an alarming rate. We have fifty years' worth of old junk crammed into our building. It's time to fight back. Our mission is to find and throw out everything we don't need." The pastor was right. So, trash bags in hand, the congregation took up his challenge and marched forward.

Eagle-eyed members found torn easy chairs, cracked dishes, and mysterious spoons of unknown origin. And who can forget the boxes of unidentified cords and cables?

Nursery toys with missing parts? A broken TV? What a disorganized mess.

The effort paid off. Scruffy items vanished, leaving tidy closets, and neatly arranged shelves. The church looked fresh, friendly, and inviting.

Our lives are a lot like that church. We've spent years accumulating a ton of things. Some lie around our houses. Some lie around our minds. Unfortunately, many of them are no longer useful. In fact, they're in our way and hindering our progress. It's time to tackle these leftover odds and ends.

Disposing of worn-out socks and chipped glassware is simple. But dealing with emotional baggage is tougher. We cling to familiar habits and ways of thinking, recycling them over and over. They served us once, but no more. We're wiser now.

This mishmash in our souls must go. But how? Jesus is a great clutter buster. He offers love and compassion, plus a shovel to dig out. Side by side, we'll get the job done.

*Do you not know that you are God's temple and that God's Spirit dwells in you?*
*1 Corinthians 3:16*

## You Always Matter

Hurtful emotional patterns have been such a struggle. They kept me safe in childhood and I assumed they always would. But that isn't true. To heal old wounds and move on, I need a different reaction to today's dilemmas. I'm thankful for new opportunities and daily chances to grow.

Perhaps you are, too. Change is not easy, and letting go of inner turmoil is tough. But just imagine how light and free you'll feel when the weight is gone. You can do it.

## Ponder and Pray

Do you hold on to thoughts or reactions that aren't helpful?

What's stopping you from releasing them?

How could Jesus lend a hand?


*Lord, I'm so overwhelmed by the clutter in my life. All this stuff, whether in my home or in my heart, needs to go. That's why I am getting rid of anything that hampers our peaceful, happy bond. Let's clean house together. Amen.*

# Leave It in the Road
## Reflection 12

*A time to seek, and a time to lose; a time to keep, and a time to cast away.  Ecclesiastes 3:6*

Any opera fans out there? Definitely! Our numbers are few, but we're a loyal bunch, always on the lookout for creative new productions. At its premiere, *Fire Shut Up in My Bones* tackled today's thorny issues with a powerful and distinctive voice.

Charles, a young black man, struggled with poverty, prejudice, and abuse. Angry and confused, he longed for a better future. As he plotted revenge against those who wronged him, many loved ones urged him to "leave it in the road." They saw the emotional and physical toll of his struggle and agreed on this advice: release your bitterness, drop your burdens, and move ahead.

We also wrestle with our inner messages. It's true that we've experienced our fair share of suffering. But what should we do? Continue to punish others or even ourselves? Seems a rather unappealing choice. Instead, let's stop, shift gears, and cast off the pain.

This is a tough decision. Yet, with help and encouragement, we can carve out a different path. The way forward may appear rocky at first, but that sure beats ruminating on unpleasant memories. Leaving it in the road might be our best option.

So, take courage. Change is possible and a new beginning lies ahead. In fact, Jesus is standing in the distance, ready to guide us on a sacred journey of healing.

*Remember not the former things, nor consider the things of old. Behold, I am doing a new thing; now it springs forth, do you not perceive it?  Isaiah 43:18-19a*

## You Always Matter

Troubling thoughts are hard to shake off. Believe me, I know. It's not easy to understand why things happened the way they did. But replaying such questions over and over won't fix the hurt. Today, I will put this darkness behind me as I step into the sunlight of God's love and support. A fresh start awaits.

And you? Don't let sadness and confusion diminish your life. Jesus opens a vista of hope just for you. Do you have the grit to walk into it? You bet.

## Ponder and Pray

Is it difficult for you to move on from prior problems? When?

What could you do differently?

Where do you perceive God in your situation?


*Lord, I feel stuck. No matter where I turn, old wounds pop up. I can't seem to avoid them. Or can I? You've mapped out an awesome path for me. Let's explore it together as the past fades away. Amen.*

# Easy Does It
## Reflection 13

*Let not your hearts be troubled, neither let them be afraid.  John 14:27b*

Birthdays kept coming. I kept aging. No wonder I heard the clock ticking on my lifelong dream of studying classical guitar. I knew nothing about the instrument, except that it sounded cool on the radio. I'm not talking about rock or folk music. Classical guitars date back hundreds of years, and the technique is tricky.

Given my background as an orchestral musician, I figured this would be a breeze and I was only weeks away from becoming a virtuoso. Wrong. I struggled with my new guitar. It felt awkward to handle, and I progressed at a snail's pace.

So, I went online and found an awesome teacher. "Hold your hands softly," he advised. "Don't clench them. And please don't strangle your guitar." His tips came in handy as I continued practicing, improving every day. I may not be the best player, but Caprice, my sweet guitar, has become a delightful companion.

How does this musical adventure relate to real life? We may tend to cling tightly to those around us. Or we might grip problems with all our strength, never releasing them. No matter the situation, it's important to ask: are we strangling our lives?

It's time to embrace life gently. As we let go, our vision clears and our energy returns. Growth, healing, and connection bring lightness and freedom to our souls.

And remember that extra special perk—plenty of space for God.

*Do not be anxious about anything, but in everything by prayer and supplication with thanksgiving let your requests be made known to God.  Philippians 4:6*

## You Always Matter

Tough situations often get the better of me. But why? Maybe because I hold them too close, losing touch with my true self. Letting go is hard, but I know I must. Today, I'll step aside and allow events to unfold on their own. When I lay my issues at God's feet, they become his responsibility. I can relax and take a break.

Why not try this yourself? Don't strangle your troubles—release them. Just march up to the altar, give them to Jesus, and you'll be free. He's waiting there for you.

## Ponder and Pray

Have you ever clung to a challenging situation? What was it?

What stopped you from releasing it?

Imagine Jesus taking charge. How would you feel?


*Lord, I'm not the most easy-going person. In fact, I stick like glue to any dilemma, and it's suffocating my spirit. Help me open my soul and watch my burdens fly to your loving heart. Amen.*

# Slippery Slope
## Reflection 14

*You have made known to me the paths of life; you will make me full of gladness with your presence.  Acts 2:28*

Today was the day. Breathless and eager, she arrived at the resort. Here she was, a 60-year-old newbie, ready for her first ski adventure. After a short lesson on the bunny slope, she hopped on the chairlift to begin her ascent up the peak.

But as she neared the crest of the mountain, her body froze with fear. The course was steep and packed with trees. Her ears filled with the imaginary crunch of snapping bones. In a panic-stricken second, she regretted her risky choice.

Sound familiar? We've all been there—whether on the ski slope or in everyday life. Exciting ideas flood our minds, and we plunge right in. But we're unprepared and confused about how to proceed. If we press ahead anyway, dire consequences could be in store.

Let's put on the brakes as we ponder these words of wisdom. "We may stand at the top of a slope, but skiing down is optional."

Excellent advice, especially when we face a sticky situation. Maybe we made a hasty decision without considering the outcome. As our plans unravel, dark thoughts of pain and distress fill our hearts. Why not pause and consider a different option? There's no shame in changing course.

Whenever we are tempted to ski down a questionable slope, let's stop and look for Jesus. He isn't at the base of the hill. No, he's standing there beside us, pointing to a better way. Why not follow his lead?

*When I thought, "My foot slips," your steadfast love, O Lord, held me up.  Psalm 94:18*

## You Always Matter

I keep finding myself in scenarios I'm not equipped to handle. Why? Probably because they are so enticing. But danger lurks in their shadow, and I need to change direction. Do I have the strength this time? Will I avoid the slippery slope? Yes, and yes.

And so can you. You are worth much more than a perilous ride down a needless hill. Before you slide down the mountain again, check your alternatives. Jesus longs to ski with you to a lovely destination. You're safe with him.

## Ponder and Pray

Have you gone down slippery slopes you know you shouldn't? When?

How could you avoid this?

In what ways is Jesus offering help?

*Lord, no matter how hard I try, I'm still drawn to those dubious decisions. But healthier choices are out there. So, let's make a U-turn. Show me your loving guidance as we explore a fresh path together. Amen.*

# Give Up the Game
## Reflection 15

*Walk in a manner worthy of the Lord, fully pleasing to him: bearing fruit in every good work and increasing in the knowledge of God.*
*Colossians 1:10*

"Just because you're winning the game doesn't mean you should keep playing."
Anonymous

We've seen this scenario in countless films and TV shows. An actor walks into a casino and begins to gamble, visions of big bucks dancing in his head. On a hot streak, he rakes in loads of chips.

But then his luck runs out as game after game goes awry. He continues to bet and loses every time, unable to walk away. Finally, the last chip slips from his hand. He leaves no better off than when he arrived.

Okay. A gambler isn't the best spiritual example. But the point remains. We begin an exciting pursuit and enjoy some success. Later we press on, not realizing our actions are no longer fruitful. We think we are winning, but we aren't. We're simply on autopilot.

Everyday activities, hopes and dreams, even heroic quests can be worthwhile. Yet questions are in order. Why are we doing this? How does it affect our lives and relationships? Is it worth our effort? What are the upsides? The downsides? Are we able to stop?

Our answers may be based on sound reasoning. Or they could reflect old wounds that still hold sway over our hearts.

Regardless, it's time to chat with Jesus about what we do and why. With patience and compassion, he always guides us on the right path.

*Trust in the Lord with all your heart, and do not lean on your own understanding. In all your ways acknowledge him, and he will make straight your paths.  Proverbs 3:5-6*

## You Always Matter

I should have stopped playing certain games ages ago. Instead, I repeated the same behaviors again and again. Why? My flawed reactions to past hurts kept me stuck in a painful history. Summoning my courage, I broke free and altered my course. A peaceful and fulfilling journey awaited me.

What about you? Do you use the same game plan over and over, even when it fails? Why not pause and consult Jesus? His advice will set you in the fast lane toward healing.

**Ponder and Pray**

Do you cling to thoughts and acts that work against you? When?

Why do you believe this happens?

How could God support your growth and change?

*Lord, I'm struggling to let go of mindless responses that hinder my well-being. I'd love to swap out my reality for a shiny new healed one. Help me give up the game. Amen.*

# Pick-Up Sticks
## Reflection 16

*Let us test and examine our ways, and return to the Lord!  Lamentations 3:40*

I have fond memories of playing pick-up sticks as a child. It was so much fun and provided endless entertainment at my grandmother's house.

The game is simple and requires only a set of plastic sticks in bright, vibrant colors. To begin, hold all of them tightly in your fist. As you release your grip, they will scatter on the table.

To win, you must take as many sticks as possible from the pile. But you can't disturb any other sticks while you do this. It's a challenge. Yet, as you lift one, you might spy another ready to be rescued.

So it is with us. We may find ourselves caught in a tangle of annoying issues. Will we ever be free? Yes, a single stick at a time. Remember, releasing the first one opens options to remove a second or even a third. Each picked up stick is a breakthrough.

And here's the bonus. As we address our difficulties, those who love us may see a change. Because of our example, they could discover new hope while gathering their own sticks.

Picking up the sticks in our lives is a delicate art. Shaky fingers struggle to liberate each pesky stick. But that's where God comes in. Why not let his steady hand guide us as sticks fly off the pile? We'll tackle obstacles we never imagined as he beams with delight.

*Let your hand be ready to help me, for I have chosen your precepts.  Psalm 119:173*

## You Always Matter

I hate being trapped in a situation with no escape. Whichever path I try, roadblocks pop up, hindering my progress. It seems like stubborn, intractable problems surround me. Or do they? If I make even a slight shift, a fresh opening appears. Then another. And another. At long last, a new perspective emerges, and my problem is solved.

You might think challenges surround you from every angle. But they don't, because Jesus is standing by. Put your hand in his. Together, you'll clear away every stick on the way to a bright future.

## Ponder and Pray

When have you felt trapped in troubles?

What specific changes did you make?

How did you sense God leading you?


*Lord, some days I'm buried under a pile of pick-up sticks and can't seem to break free. I am totally stuck. But is that true? Whenever I pick up one stick, another becomes available. Help me see my next move. Be with me now and forever. Amen.*

# Backpacking

## Reflection 17

*May the Lord give strength to his people! May the Lord bless his people with peace!*
*Psalm 29:11*

The pastor was beyond tired. Day after day, he visited the sick, wrote sermons, attended church meetings, and helped in the soup kitchen. The sheer number of responsibilities and people in distress sapped his energy. It was enough to overwhelm even the strongest clergy.

But this minister hid a clever secret—an invisible, imaginary backpack. No one saw the bag slung across his shoulders. Whenever he confronted an unsolvable problem, he put it in the pack. Whenever criticism stung his heart, he put it in the pack. Whenever exhaustion threatened to stop him, he put it in the pack.

Eventually, the pack became too cumbersome to lift. But this wise pastor had a plan. Calming his soul in a quiet corner of the church, he imagined slipping off the straps as he laid the backpack close to Jesus. "I've carried these troubles long enough so I'm handing them over. They're yours now." Free of his burden, he relaxed, eager to take up his mission again.

This could be us. We haul around sorrow and misery, possibly for decades. Worries weigh down our souls and dampen our spirits. Understandably, we feel inferior and less than. But the answer is always available. Let's place our problems in God's hands and hand over our backpacks. As he graciously accepts them, joy, calm, and freedom lift our hearts once more.

*Return, O my soul, to your rest; for the Lord has dealt bountifully with you.  Psalm 116:7*

## You Always Matter

Some days are too much to handle. Truthfully, it's more like weeks, months, or years. Perhaps life takes a wrong turn, old hurts bubble up, or simple conversations become harsh. No wonder I'm crushed and demoralized. It's comforting to know that Jesus is always there, ready to help. As I lay my concerns on his altar, the load lightens and all is well.

Maybe your life is the same. Why let your spirit sag under a heavy weight? You don't need to. Just hand your backpack to God. He's strong and delighted to carry the burden for you.

## Ponder and Pray

Do you hold on to hurt and pain? When?

What could convince you to relinquish it?

How can Jesus encourage you?


*Lord, the world is too overwhelming. Arrows hit me from every direction, and I don't know what to do. That's why I'm so happy you're with me. Help me release my many burdens. Here's my backpack—please take it. I am thrilled to give the load back to you. Amen.*

# Lost and Found
## Reflection 18

*The Lord is my shepherd; I shall not want.*
*Psalm 23:1*

"I'm all alone and it's getting dark. Nobody saw me fall into the ravine—not even my mother. That was hours ago. My voice is rough and raspy from yelling. I can't crawl out because my leg is swollen and bleeding. Everything hurts and I'm scared. Help!"

Despair overwhelmed the little lamb as her plight grew desperate. Suddenly, a shadow appeared over the canyon. Her shepherd had arrived to rescue her. He climbed down and hoisted the tiny sheep over his shoulders, carrying her to safety. She sighed, relaxing in his strong, tender embrace.

Who among us hasn't experienced a similar situation? Life's challenges seem unbearable. We try our best, but time after time we stumble into a hole. Peering around, we find no friendly arm to lift us out. Then Jesus appears.

So, remember this. We don't need to be perfect. We don't need to solve every problem that comes our way. And we don't even need to climb out of whatever pit we've fallen into. All we need is to be found. That's it. And here's the good news. Jesus is looking. He's always looking.

He yearns for us when we're lost and won't stop searching until he finds all who are missing. As he gently picks us up, we nestle into his arms. With a light and joyful step, Jesus carries us home.

*Rejoice with me, for I have found my sheep that was lost.  Luke 15:6b*

## You Always Matter

It's so easy to fall into a hole. I've done it. We've all done it. The challenge is getting back out, especially if nobody knows where I am. That's why I'm glad Jesus is watching out for me. No matter what happens, I won't stay lost for long. He's always there, ready to scoop me up and keep me safe.

And what about you? No matter how adrift or alone you may be, your difficulties are short-lived. Jesus and his giant binoculars are on the lookout. You're never forgotten.

## Ponder and Pray

Have you ever felt trapped in a pit and nobody noticed? When?

How did it work out?

In what ways did you sense God's hand guiding you?

*Lord, I can relate to the little sheep. It's scary to be all alone in a deep hole. But here's the truth—I'm not alone. You always come and save the day. It may not be the way I expect. But your strong arm will pull me to safety. Stay with me today, tomorrow, and forever. Amen.*

# Tree Troubles

## Reflection 19

*This is my comfort in my affliction, that your promise gives me life.  Psalm 119:50*

Our side yard remains unfenced. The prior owner enclosed the back but left an open area to welcome wildlife visitors. Even though we live in the city, small groups of deer often pass through. Such is our Colorado home.

Last year we decided to spiff up the deer pasture a bit by adding a couple of trees. All summer long they were leafy and green. Then cooler weather arrived, and with it the season for antler mishaps.

As winter drew near, we noticed a "buck rub" or gash on one of the saplings. A male deer had vigorously rubbed his head against the trunk, causing noticeable damage. We feared the worst.

We gently wrapped our little tree in a special coat to keep it safe and warm. Would it make it through the frosty months? When spring came, we removed the covering, crossing our fingers for a miracle. Soon, tiny green leaves danced on every branch. Our tree was saved.

The spiritual life is similar. Everybody faces tough challenges—nobody is immune. Difficulties bring intense pain and trauma while our fears multiply. What if the hurt doesn't heal? Can we handle such heartbreak? When will we recover?

But time passes, and our healing begins. Soon new tissue is growing around the sore spot. Our skin might appear rough, and the scar might persist. Yet our recovery is sweet, indeed. God has touched our souls.

*For I will restore health to you, and your wounds I will heal, declares the Lord.  Jeremiah 30:17a*

## You Always Matter

Like that injured tree, I wonder if my soul will ever mend. Most days I'm okay, but when old wounds flare up, I feel lost once more. Who is there to lend a hand? Who is there to envelop me in cozy comfort? I am so glad a special someone always stands ready to offer compassion and concern. It's Jesus.

What about you? Life can be a tiresome slog. But consider how far you've come. Progress may be slow, your path wavy, but new shoots are sprouting. Keep walking. God is with you.

## Ponder and Pray

Recall an instance when an emotional wound troubled you. What was it?

Were you able to get better? How?

Where was God with you in this?

*Lord, unfortunate things happen to me, as they do to everyone. But being trapped in my anguish is no fun. Just like that little tree, I need your special coat. Protect and nurture me as fresh growth emerges, and I am restored. Amen.*

# Let There Be Light
## Reflection 20

*The light shines in the darkness, and the darkness has not overcome it.  John 1:5*

Darkness engulfed her. Frightened and unsure, she stepped out of her stranded car. With no streetlights for guidance, she fumbled her way along the deserted country road. At last, a farmhouse came into view. Though the windows were closed and draped, a faint glimmer of light slipped through. She pressed on.

Suddenly, a door flew open, light flooding the twilight sky. The darkness vanished, revealing a clear path ahead. No longer stumbling, she was safe. Help was at hand.

Nice story—but why do we care? Perhaps because it contains an important message. Light flowed from the farmhouse, brightening the landscape. Darkness didn't walk into the house and carve out a space. This was a one-way transaction. Light had the power and darkness could not overcome it.

So it is with us. Some days are great. Other days, not so much. We feel down and dejected. Gloom and rejection lurk in every corner. Darkness envelopes our world, leaving no trace of light in our lives. Will our troubles ever end? Do we matter at all?

Yes, and yes. It's time to shine a flashlight on our situation. As the path becomes clear, our problems seem less overwhelming. Even a small beam of light defeats the darkness. Jesus is our farmhouse by the road. Nothing can diminish his radiance. Why not bask in the glow of his light today?

*And God said, "Let there be light," and there was light.  Genesis 1:3*

## You Always Matter

This is a comforting story. The light wins and the darkness doesn't. No matter what gets me down, the light will win. Regardless of the obstacles in my way, the light will win. Even when I feel lost and insignificant, the light will win. This may not happen right away. But someday Jesus will validate my efforts, even if no one else does.

So, take courage. Whatever your struggle, whatever your darkness, it will fade away. A light WILL shine on your path. The darkness WILL disappear. You WILL know your worth.

## Ponder and Pray

Do you recall a time when you felt dejected or when everything went wrong? Describe.

Would shedding a bit of light on the issue make a difference?

How might Jesus help illuminate the problem?

*Lord, some days life seems black. I don't see a way out. I'm stuck and I can't find an answer. But then I remember you. The world looks better with even a tiny sliver of your light. Let me delight in your radiance forever. Amen.*

# Uniquely You
**Reflection 21**

*As each has received a gift, use it to serve one another, as good stewards of God's varied grace.  1 Peter 4:10*

"Hmmm...what an interesting offer. Should I take it? Am I qualified? And whose idea was this, anyway?"

Scrolling through her email one day, she found a message from a ministry several hundred miles away. Seems they had heard about her local work and wanted her to join their team. How flattering. But a nagging voice inside questioned her ability. Surely, such an overwhelming proposal was beyond her. Plus, she loved her current job and didn't want to leave. Should she stay or should she go?

She prayed for guidance and consulted a couple of trusted friends. After careful consideration, they agreed on their advice. "Stay put. God wants you here." This offer wasn't for her.

Such a familiar tale. Why do we doubt ourselves? Why do we assume that cool opportunities are only for the super spiritual? Or for famous leaders? Or for anybody but us? They aren't. But that doesn't mean every assignment has our name on it either.

In God's operating system, everyone has a talent. Everyone has a purpose. We're all here for a reason. And who knows? Perhaps we are fulfilling his vision right now without even realizing it.

So, what do we bring to the table? And which table is ours? We might be unsure, but our loved ones know the answers. With their support, we will develop an accurate snapshot. And don't forget Jesus. He holds the crucial vote.

*For the gifts and the calling of God are irrevocable. Romans 11:29*

## You Always Matter

Some days, I wonder if I have anything meaningful to offer. Is there a place for my gifts? Is my reality too small? Maybe I sell myself short. Like everyone else, I am blessed with unique talents. My life matters, whether I'm exactly where Jesus wants me or if a change is on the horizon. Who I am makes a difference.

And what about you? God has given you special abilities to serve others. And somebody out there needs you. So don't hold back. Be bold—you've got what it takes.

## Ponder and Pray

Have you been uncertain about your gifts and where to use them? Is this realistic?

How could you discover the truth?

What does Jesus say?


*Lord, you know I struggle. Do I belong? What are my talents? Am I too critical? You crafted a one-of-a-kind plan for me, and the ability to live it. I'm ready to embark on the journey set out for me. Let's get moving. Amen.*

# Last Can of Soup
## Reflection 22

*You keep him in perfect peace whose mind is stayed on you, because he trusts in you.*
*Isaiah 26:3*

What if I run out of money? I mean literally run out—without any left? I'm embarrassed to admit I struggle with this even today. Every so often, my mind fills with haunting memories, like the time I had to buy luggage decades ago.

My election to the Colorado Springs City Council meant business trips were on the horizon. But my banged up, worn-out, super-heavy suitcases would never do.

Clearly, I needed to invest in new travel bags.

I found a cute little set on sale for $100. But I've always had a fear of spending money. Was I certain I could afford it? To find out, I spent days adding up everything I owned—checking account, savings, car, house, and who knows what. Obviously, the total was a lot more than $100. Whew! I was relieved and soon tucked my new luggage into the closet.

Yes, this was overkill and rather silly. But money fears remain a challenge. For example, I'm terrified of getting down to my last can of soup. That's why I always keep a few in the pantry, so I won't starve. Am I nuts?

How often do we needlessly stress about situations that are just fine? Perhaps we lack confidence in ourselves and God. Here's a better plan. Let go of obsessions, grasp his hand, and move ahead. We have enough.

*And the peace of God, which surpasses all understanding, will guard your hearts and your minds in Christ Jesus.  Philippians 4:7*

## You Always Matter

My dread of running out of something crucial continues to torment me. What if I starve to death? What if I can't afford to live? Although this might seem extreme, I find it terrifying. Trust lies at the heart of the issue. God created me with infinite value, the smarts to survive, and the guts to do it. Today's the day to believe him.

The same applies to you. The fear of scarcity and loss can be overwhelming. But take courage. Jesus holds you safely in the palm of his hand. Nothing bad will happen.

## Ponder and Pray

Do you cringe in terror at the thought of a particular scenario? What is it?

How realistic is that?

In what ways could God help you face this fear?


*Lord, irrational worry sometimes gets the best of me. I know everything is fine, but doubt drags me down. Wrap your arms around me and help me feel secure. With you, I have all I need. Amen.*

# Night Light

**Reflection 23**

*The Lord is my light and my salvation; whom shall I fear? Psalm 27:1a*

Terror gripped him as the war raged on. The little guy, only six years old, had seen both parents killed. He survived and somehow found his way to a cold, dark basement crammed with strangers.

Food was scarce, and the adults seemed anxious and distracted. Older kids mocked and ridiculed him. He felt so hungry he even tried to eat his only toy.

After weeks of suffering, a kindly couple took the young boy to their home in a different city. Here he was safe and warm, with plenty to eat. But the conflict continued, and his new family endured frequent blackouts. The sudden darkness terrified him, but the lights soon flickered on again.

As the months went by, his soul healed as fear faded away. One day he said to his new mother, "I'm not afraid of the dark anymore. The light always comes back on."

What about you and me? In times of despair, we question if hope will ever return. We feel overwhelmed by anxiety, convinced our lives will never improve. We're stuck and going nowhere.

But that's not true. We will heal, trust once more, and move forward. As we do, let's also seek helpful allies to join in this journey. And remember, our very best cheerleader is Jesus himself. Look, there he is, beckoning us from darkness into his light.

*For it is you who light my lamp; the Lord my God lightens my darkness.  Psalm 18:28*

## You Always Matter

What a terrifying situation. Yet not only did this child survive, but he thrived when brought to safety. Perhaps this was the legacy of his deceased parents. Did they instill a sense of worth in their son? Was he aware, even at a young age, that his life had value? Was this the source of his incredible endurance? We'll never know.

But why not follow his example? You may believe the darkness will persist forever. It won't. Don't let gloom overshadow your spirit. Have faith in yourself, take God's hand, and walk into the light.

## Ponder and Pray

Have you faced dire circumstances that never seemed to end? Describe.

As the situation resolved, what glimmers of light did you see?

How can you use this experience to enhance your confidence in Jesus?

*Lord, when difficult things happen, I am certain I will never be okay again. But we both know that isn't true. I'm still here on earth for a reason. You'll never give up on me, so I won't either. Amen.*

# Letting Go
## Reflection 24

*Weeping may tarry for the night, but joy comes with the morning.  Psalm 30:5b*

"When people walk away from you, let them go. Your destiny is never tied to anyone who leaves you, and it doesn't mean they are bad people. It just means that their part in your story is over." T.D. Jakes

Ouch. When a person's departure creates a gaping hole in my world, I fill it with grief. Why can't everyone stay connected forever, like a big, happy family? Yes, I know this is not possible. Or even desirable.

Sometimes friends and acquaintances grow apart. It's nobody's fault. Recently, I sorted through some old files. Familiar names popped up that I hadn't seen in years. I wondered where they were now.

Folks may leave for reasons that have nothing to do with us. Perhaps a friend or loved one is struggling with an issue and believes the solution lies elsewhere. We didn't cause it. We're not bad. We're not the problem.

Yet, rather than letting go, we tie our emotions to those who left our story ages ago. In their absence, they hold an outsized position in our minds and hearts. We need to admit that their role in our history is over.

Our destiny belongs to us and to God. Even though someone has strayed from our orbit, let's keep our eyes on Jesus. With him, our lives will write a captivating tale of love.

*When the cares of my heart are many, your consolations cheer my soul.  Psalm 94:19*

## You Always Matter

Acknowledging that I'm okay and my life matters is the hardest part of moving on. Instead, I obsess over my mistakes and brainstorm ways to fix the situation. But it may be beyond repair. It's time to stop my fault-finding and extend a little grace. Just because a relationship didn't work doesn't mean I am bad.

And what about you? Despite your tears, can you accept that you are good? Can you move ahead to fulfill your potential as a person and child of God? After all, that's who you are. Don't forget it.

## Ponder and Pray

Have you ever struggled to walk forward when a relationship ended? Describe.

What helped you find healing and remember your own goodness?

How did you sense God's presence, reassuring and leading you?

*Lord, losing a special someone causes such a void. I often blame myself, regardless of reality. What went wrong? Could I have prevented this? It's time to trust that their choices aren't always about me. Please comfort my soul as you guide me along your sacred path. Amen.*

# Will You Marry Me?
## Reflection 25

*The Lord is good to those who wait for him, to the soul who seeks him.  Lamentations 3:25*

Long, long ago, when I was young and at least reasonably attractive, men began buzzing around. Not hordes of them, mind you. To be honest, the cast of characters was rather small, mostly just friends. But a few had potential.

In those earlier years, I received several marriage proposals. As I look back, they all had one feature in common. All I cared about was whether each man liked me. What I thought about him seemed irrelevant.

My task became to morph into the girl these suitors wanted. I set my personal identity aside as I focused on being "good enough." But were they suitable for me? Sadly, my radar let me down on this question.

Today I see my faulty logic as vital questions went unanswered. Who were these people? What were their interests? How about their strengths and flaws? To me, men were all alike and interchangeable, like spare parts. It made no difference who I chose. I knew we could create a happy life together. What a recipe for disaster.

God sees each person as a unique and precious soul. But when we twist ourselves into a pretzel for a questionable relationship, how can he guide us?

Sometimes we are blind to the reality in front of our eyes. Before we make a huge mistake, let's remove our blinders and ask, "Hey Jesus. Where are we going? Show us the way."

*I will instruct you and teach you in the way you should go; I will counsel you with my eye upon you.  Psalm 32:8*

## You Always Matter

Do all men make equally good husbands? Must I change myself to find a mate? Both questions are ridiculous. But back then, I didn't think I mattered. Only my prospective partner was important. Today, it's clear that my reasoning was flawed. Making wise choices and staying true to myself is essential. That's the key to a successful marriage.

What about you? Have you ever gone to extremes to reinvent yourself for a relationship? If so, don't do it again. Jesus knows you're worth more than that—and so do I. Trust us.

## Ponder and Pray

When did you compromise yourself to please someone? Describe.

Given a second chance, how would you act differently?

What message do you hear from God about this?


*Lord, relationship trauma is tiresome. I'm so glad that I recognize my value today. Help me continue to improve my choices as I become my authentic self. Amen.*

# New Beginnings

**Reflection 26**

*The steadfast love of the Lord never ceases; his mercies never come to an end.*
*Lamentations 3:22*

Grief poured from the tiny chapel. Folks had gathered to honor a young mother, taken too soon. Her husband and children were shattered. Others were heartbroken at the passing of a good and loyal friend.

As the service progressed, the pastor's sermon took an unexpected turn. "God is with us in beginnings and endings. A chapter never really closes because it's also the dawn of a different story. Even death is a resurrection. God goes with us through endings to new beginnings."

As we grapple with affliction, finding anything positive is tough. We lost someone or something important, so we're angry and upset. We didn't ask for this situation, and we struggle to find our way. That's why walking toward a fresh start takes openness, trust, and a ton of courage.

Perhaps it helps to understand that every tragedy has a second side, painful as it may be. The end of a relationship marks the birth of another opportunity. Even the loss of a beloved pet could lead to surprising possibilities. Though shrouded in mist today, the road ahead awaits our discovery.

Remember the pastor's words. God is with us through all our beginnings and endings, openings and closings. With tender care, he leads us from one place to the next, offering unwavering support and kindness. Don't fear an ending, however difficult it seems. Look, a new season is unfolding. Welcome it.

*It is the Lord who goes before you. He will be with you; he will not leave you or forsake you. Deuteronomy 31:8a*

## You Always Matter

Endings are hard. They feel final, and I feel lost. How can I go on? What's left for me? Who will care? New beginnings are tough too since I can't see the path forward. Will my journey be worth it? Will I be happy again? Yes, and yes. I just need to unclench my fist to let God in.

It's the same for you. What lies in store is a mystery. You might be unsure. You might even stumble and fall. Yet Jesus will lovingly guide you into the next season of life.

## Ponder and Pray

When have you faced a difficult loss? Describe.

Were you able to move through it to hopeful new horizons? How?

Where did you sense God's presence, gently encouraging you?


*Lord, I don't want anything in my world to change. Never, never, ever. Okay, I know I'm unrealistic and probably too dramatic. Stay by my side as we face life's challenges together. Amen.*

# Open the Cage
## Reflection 27

*For I know the plans I have for you, declares the Lord, plans for welfare and not for evil, to give you a future and a hope.  Jeremiah 29:11*

"Some birds are not meant to be caged, that's all. Their feathers are too bright, their songs too sweet and wild. So you let them go, or when you open the cage to feed them, they somehow fly out past you. And the part of you that knows it was wrong to imprison them in the first place rejoices, but still, the place where you live is that much more drab and empty for their departure." Stephen King

A gloomy thought—or perhaps not.

If we're the bird, our newfound freedom is intoxicating. At last, we can embrace the life God intended for us.

If we're the human, it's complicated. We're thrilled to watch our beloved bird soar higher and higher, free of its dreary cage. Yet, our hearts ache because our feathered friend brought joy to our lives. Now its chirpy energy is gone, leaving a gaping hole.

No matter where we stand, possibilities and challenges await. Will we have the faith to spread our wings and be ourselves? Or do we have the compassion to support a loved one in their quest for self-discovery?

Our best response is to trust Jesus. Whether we're the bird or the human, he's got a plan. So take a break. Rest in his hand as you scan the horizon. Opportunities abound.

*Commit your work to the Lord, and your plans will be established.  Proverbs 16:3*

**You Always Matter**

This story depicts two sides of the same coin. Both are possible. Both are a stretch. Do I have what it takes to open my wings and soar, or will my doubts hold me back? On the flip side, can I release those I love to fulfill their destinies, even if I'm left alone? I know the answer. By myself, maybe not—with God, absolutely.

The same is true for you. Why not gather your courage, take God's hand, and move forward? Whichever way he sends you, whichever way you choose, it's the right way.

**Ponder and Pray**

Have you faced issues while pursuing your dreams or supporting others in theirs? Describe.

How did the situation ultimately resolve?

Where did you see Jesus in your dilemma?

*Lord, life is such a struggle. Achieving my goals or inspiring others to do so seems daunting. But there is a blueprint for everyone. Give me the strength to boldly follow your lead, no matter what. Amen.*

# Planting Flowers
## Reflection 28

*Let your light shine before others, so that they may see your good works and give glory to your Father who is in heaven.  Matthew 5:16*

I was a latecomer to Christianity. My path to Jesus was full of zigs and zags, including an unusual conversion experience and tons of "remedial" theology. Eventually I became a Christian and joined a church. I was 41.

The senior pastor invited all the new members to a dessert reception on a frosty winter evening. I still remember his words. "Each one of you is God's flower. Don't seek exotic soil or an eye-catching garden. Just bloom where you are planted."

Fair enough. But an exotic spiritual life sounds so...exotic. How exciting to minister in Tahiti. Or serve the poor in Africa. But leaving our familiar world behind can be tough. Plus, foreign ministry isn't a good fit for everyone. Whether we're native plants or transplants, we can do valuable work anywhere. Jesus has gifted each of us with special talents. We just need to use them no matter where we are.

Clear-eyed trust in God's leading is a must. We should walk the center line, not underestimating our skills, but not exaggerating them either. And neither should we forget the genuine needs in our own backyards. There's plenty to do wherever we are planted.

It's time to open our eyes and listen to the pastor. We have so many ways to serve. Pick one and start blooming.

*For God is not unjust so as to overlook your work and the love that you have shown for his name in serving the saints, as you still do.*
*Hebrews 6:10*

## You Always Matter

Am I truly able to bloom where I'm planted? Or should I try somewhere else? Sometimes I feel uncertain, especially when my confidence dwindles. Yet when I consider a change, I realize this is silly. Jesus put me here for a purpose—to do as much good as I can for as long as I can.

Your life is the same. You may think you have nothing to offer. So, check your vision. It might be a bit cloudy. God sees your abilities, as do countless others. So, show us your blooms.

## Ponder and Pray

Have you ever wondered if the ministry grass is greener somewhere else? Describe.

How could you contribute to your own community?

Where do you believe God wants you to be?


*Lord, sometimes I am clueless about what you expect from me. Maybe I'm just not listening. But I know this—the soil beneath me is perfect. So, plant me today. Amen.*

# Stuck in the Past

## Reflection 29

*Forgetting what lies behind and straining forward to what lies ahead, I press on toward the goal for the prize of the upward call of God in Christ Jesus.  Philippians 3:13b-14*

Hordes of flies buzzed around the church, circling perilously close to the communion table. They were annoying and a health hazard, too. To keep these pesky critters at bay, the pastor covered the chalice with a small white cloth.

Fast forward 100 years. The insect issue was solved decades ago, yet the current pastor still covers the chalice. At one point, he tried to explain that the cloth wasn't necessary.

But his flock wouldn't hear of it. "We've always done it this way. Don't mess with our tradition."

Sound familiar? Chances are we have a few outdated traditions ourselves. What about the heaping bowl of ice cream we enjoy every night before bed? That was a delightful treat during our 20s. But if we're trying to lose 25 pounds in middle age, it's a problem. Life has changed.

Letting go of deeply ingrained habits isn't easy. They tug at our hearts. Perhaps they even shielded us from harm and kept us safe long ago. But we live in today's world. It's time to free ourselves from the emotional baggage of the past.

Why settle for the not-so-good old days? A dawn filled with promise and hope has arrived. As we create fresh traditions, yesterday's choices will fade into the mist.

Let's take God's hand and walk together into a bright future.

*Behold, I am making all things new.*
*Revelation 21:5a*

## You Always Matter

Even today, I deal with thoughts and behaviors that are no longer helpful. Once upon a time, they were my protectors and guardians. That was then, and this is now. Yet, when I try to set them aside, these traditions sneak back in when I least expect them. This effort is an ongoing project between Jesus and me.

This applies to you, too. God is standing by, ready to help. Let him bring your body and spirit into loving balance, free from the burdens of the past. You deserve it.

## Ponder and  Pray

Do you ever catch yourself thinking or acting in ways that work against you? When?

What steps can you take to break from tradition?

How could Jesus lend a hand?

*Lord, some of my old habits just don't cut it anymore. I'd love to put these unhelpful traditions behind me, but I need your help. Please heal my soul as you and I embrace an exciting new beginning. Amen.*

# Not Forgotten

## Reflection 30

*Fear not, for I have redeemed you; I have called you by name, you are mine.  Isaiah 43:1*

The war left nothing untouched. Bombed out apartments littered the landscape. Schools and hospitals became empty shells reduced to rubble. Even worse, enemy troops occupied the town for months, terrorizing all who remained. No place was safe. No one escaped harm.

At long last, the invaders retreated. Soon the outside world restored contact, finding a city in ruins. And a gruesome secret.

Exiled citizens cautiously made their way back home. As they walked past the crumbling buildings, a grisly sight met their eyes. Lifeless and decaying bodies covered the once lovely streets. Rather than flee their homes, these residents had stayed to fight. Tragically, they were gunned down in a senseless slaughter. How is such atrocity possible?

A solitary priest began to bury the dead. Onlookers seemed perplexed because many who perished were unidentified. How could he perform these rites, not knowing who the individuals were?

"God knows their names," he replied.

And so he does. Jesus knew each person, and he knows us. Regardless of what happens, he never forgets. Even a devastating story like this holds a kernel of hope.

We may never experience such terrifying circumstances. Yet, who among us hasn't felt alone and scared? Who hasn't longed for comfort and security in troubling times? We can find strength knowing that God is always with us. He knows our names. Our lives and legacies will endure for all eternity.

*I will not forget you. Behold, I have engraved you on the palms of my hands.  Isaiah 49:15b-16a*

## You Always Matter

My biggest fear is to be forgotten, as if I never existed. I even bought a cemetery plot near the sidewalk so visitors would see my headstone. How extreme is that? But I need not worry. God knows my name—and everything about me. My legacy is safe with him.

And so is yours. What will history remember about you? Hard to tell. But Jesus knows who you are and what you've overcome. He has engraved your name on his hands. Your value will abide forever.

## Ponder and Pray

Have you ever worried about being forgotten? When?

How did you deal with the situation and your feelings?

What part has God played in the outcome?

*Lord, I've never faced dire situations, but my reality seems so fickle. Today I'm accepted. Tomorrow I'm overlooked. Does my life count? Will anyone recall my acts of goodness? I hope so. Still, one truth is certain. You'll never forget me, no matter what. Amen.*

# Our Journey Continues
## Closing Words

*These things I have spoken to you, that my joy may be in you, and that your joy may be full.*
*John 15:11*

Dear friends, we've come a long way in a few short chapters. Together, we read stories of faith, stories of hope, and stories of love. We found encouragement and inspiration in the everyday circumstances of life.

Ours has been a tender trek, filled with insights about our lives and compassion for our struggles. Through it all, Jesus has walked by our side, rejoicing over us with singing, revealing a renewed sense of our value.

We have reached a resting place, an oasis of cool refreshment. But our adventure isn't over. Challenges remain as we mend our spirits and fortify our souls. Let's keep walking beside Jesus toward a future brimming with promise.

May we seek his hand to lead us.
May we allow his care to give us strength.
May we accept his grace as we
embrace our worth.

The Lord be with you now and always. Amen.

# Request and Invitation

Hi friend,

Thanks so much for reading *You Always Matter*. Hope you found it uplifting and encouraging.

Would you consider writing a quick review, even a sentence or two? Reviews are ever so helpful to authors like me. I invite you to post one with your favorite online bookseller today. It's super easy and only takes a couple of minutes.

I'm also delighted to invite you to subscribe to my e-newsletter. Why not enjoy a sprinkle of inspiration a few times a year. My husband and I offer this through our ministry, Spiritual Formation House.

Interested? Hop on over to MySFH.com and click the subscribe button. I'll take it from there.

Thanks again—sure appreciate you!

Lisa

# About the Author

Lisa Aré Wulf is an award-winning women's devotional author. Her print, audio, and e-books have been finalists in the USA Best Book Awards, the Independent Author Network Book of the Year Awards, the Next Generation Indie Book Awards, and the Voice Arts Awards.

Publications across the country have featured Lisa's articles on Christian living and spiritual growth. As a speaker, she shares her faith with transparency and grace.

A graduate of Fuller Theological Seminary, Lisa also holds two degrees from the University of Colorado. She is an adjunct accounting professor, owned a CPA firm, served in elected public office, and was a professional orchestral musician.

Lisa and her husband, Calvin, enjoy the mountain scenery at their Colorado home. For more information about Lisa Aré Wulf or to sign up for her e-newsletter, please visit LisaAreWulf.com.

Made in United States
Troutdale, OR
10/25/2024